The Ullswater Celebrity ⸤

is published by

Trans-Pennine Publishing Ltd.
PO Box 10
Appleby-in-Westmorland
CA16 6FA

on behalf of
'GUYS THE LIMIT'
Ullswater Community College
Wetheriggs Lane, Penrith
Cumbria CA11 8NG
01768 242160

LAYOUT AND DESIGN
'GUYS THE LIMIT'
with the assistance of
Kevin Bradley - Burwain Studios

British Cataloguing in Publication Data
A catalogue record of this book is available from the British Library
Trans-Pennine Publications ISBN 09521070 1-5

Introduction

ULLSWATER
COMMUNITY COLLEGE

There is little that is more pleasurable than enjoying food with good friends.

This fine book is brimming over with the warmth and enjoyment that comes from sharing dishes which are personal favourites.

I am very proud of the enterprise and determination by the Special Students from '*GUYS THE LIMIT* ' Team Enterprise. They will be delighted to know that you are enjoying tucking into the fruits of their hard work.

My grateful thanks to the Team Enterprise business advisors and, of course, to all the celebrities who have told us something about their secret passions.

Enjoy these truly scrumptious treats!

David Robinson
Principal

Thank you for buying this book of celebrity recipes. We are a group of Sixth Form Students from the Learning Support Department at Ullswater Community College, Penrith. The college is a large comprehensive school on the eastern side of the Lake District, only a few miles from the shores of Ullswater Lake, hence the name "*Ullswater Celebrity Cookbook*".

The idea for the book came from our involvement in Team Enterprise, a national educational charity which helps give hands-on business experience to young people.

We formed a company called 'Guys the Limit' in which we became shareholders. We also sold shares to our friends and families to raise funds to start our enterprise. We worked together as a team and all members became directors.

The team is as follows:

Nina Armstrong	Graham Fleming	Scott Morrison
Adrian Briscoe	Kevin Gough	George Park
Neil Carruthers	Helen Holliday	Graham Smith
John Cook	Shaun Jesko	Stevie Smith
Jamie Ferry	John Littlefair	Jamie Ward
		James Young

Letters were sent to people in the world of television, politics, media, sport, business and public life. They all turned out to be real super stars when they returned recipes and kind words of support.

Getting the recipes was one thing, getting a book designed and published was another, in this respect we are grateful for the expertise of those mentioned in the acknowledgments.

We learned such a lot, how to hold meetings, how to talk to each other and communicate with others! We also learnt what banks are about, how to handle accounts, what to do with money and how to get it (hard work), using computers and fax machines, finding and seeking information, attending trade fairs, and talking to advisers and customers. Most importantly, we have learnt how to be us, a team.

Enjoy your meal with the stars.

Guys the Limit

The Ullswater Celebrity Cookbook

CONTENTS

FISH PIE RECIPE
KRISS AKABUSI

2oz butter
4oz cheese
$^3/_4$ pt milk
2 fish fillets
4 large potatoes (mashed)
1 large onion (diced)
Salt to taste
Ground pepper

Poach the fish in milk and butter for 20 mins over medium heat.
Remove fish from milk cocktail.
Boil potatoes and mash.
To the milk cocktail add cheese, melt and mix.
Dice onion and add to fish.
Add milk and cheese cocktail to mashed potatoes and stir.
Place fish on the bottom of oven-proof dish and cover with mashed potatoes.
Bake in a preheated oven, 375°F/190°C/Gas 5 for 30-40 mins or until potato is crispy brown.
Serve with favourite vegetable or salad.

Enjoy!!!!

EASY LENTIL AND LEMON SOUP
FIONA ARMSTRONG

1 pint of stock (real or made with 2 vegetable cubes)
4 heaped tablespoons red lentils
Juice of half a lemon
1 small onion, diced
1 small carrot, diced
Salt and pepper

Heat the stock until boiling.
Add carrot, onions and lentils.
Simmer for 25 minutes.
Add lemon juice at the end.
Salt and pepper to taste.

CHICKEN TOSCANA
THE ARCHBISHOP OF CANTERBURY

3 lb. roasting chicken
1 onion
1 carrot
Bouquet garni
$^3/_4$ pint water
Salt and pepper
4oz mushrooms
1 small cucumber
1dessertspoon arrowroot
1 tablespoon snipped chives

Simmer the chicken gently in the water with the vegetables, herbs and seasoning until tender - about 45 to 50 minutes.

In the meantime chop the mushrooms finely, peel the cucumber and cut into quarters lengthwise and then cut into 2 inch pieces. Blanch the cucumber and drain well.
Strain the stock from the chicken when cooked and add to another saucepan. Boil the stock to reduce by about half its original quantity.

Add the mushrooms and simmer for about 3 minutes.

Take the chicken and carve into neat joints and arrange on a serving dish.

Mix the arrowroot with a little stock and add to the pan. Stir until boiling. Add the chives and cucumber. Spoon over the chicken and serve at once.

Serve with new potatoes and green vegetables.

With the Compliments of
The Chaplain
to the Archbishop of Canterbury

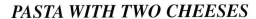
PASTA WITH TWO CHEESES
THE RT. HON. PADDY ASHDOWN MP

Serves 2

1 large tin (15 oz/375g) plum tomatoes
1 clove of garlic, chopped
1 tablespoon olive oil
2 teaspoons dried basil or five fresh basil leaves
2 oz/50g mature Cheddar cheese, grated
5 oz/125g packet Mozzarella cheese, chopped into cubes
Any sort of pasta

Put a large pan of lightly salted water on to boil.

In a heavy-based pan, mash the tomatoes with the back of a wooden spoon, add the oil, basil and garlic, and simmer gently so that the sauce thickens.

When the water boils, add the pasta, following the cooking instructions on the pack. It normally takes ten minutes for pasta to be ready.

Now add the two cheeses to the tomato sauce, turning the heat right down. Stir well once, then leave while the pasta finishes off. If the sauce starts to stick, turn off the heat and cover with a lid to keep it hot.

Once the pasta is cooked, drain well, place the tomato and cheese sauce on top and serve immediately with a crisp green salad.

CARROT AND SWEET POTATO SOUP
THE RT. HON. TONY BLAIR MP

1 medium onion
3 large carrots
1 large sweet potato
1 tablespoon chopped fresh coriander
Half a pint vegetable stock
Half a pint orange juice
Half a pint milk
1 tablespoon olive oil
Salt and freshly ground black pepper

Finely chop the vegetables and sweat in the olive oil until soft but not browned.
Add the stock and orange juice.
Simmer for half an hour.

Put in a blender and puree until smooth.
Return to pan. Add milk and reheat.

Season to taste and serve, garnish with coriander.
(If the soup is too thick use more stock.)

PLAICE PARCELS
MICHAEL BARRY

4 plaice fillets, about 100g/3 ½ oz each
125ml/ 4 fl oz Hollandaise sauce
150ml/ ¼ pint soured cream
100g/ 3 ½ oz cooked peeled prawns
2 tablespoons snipped fresh chives
serve with salt and pepper
mashed potatoes or rice
green beans
lemon wedges to serve

Preheat oven to 180C/350F/Gas 4. Cut each plaice in half lengthways. Combine Hollandaise sauce and cream, then stir half of this mixture into the prawns, use this mixture to stuff the plaice fillets: place about one and a half tablespoons on the thick end of the fillet and roll it up.

Secure with a cocktail stick and repeat with the remaining fillets.

Stand them upright on their sides in a flameproof baking dish into which they comfortably fit and season well. Spoon over the remaining Hollandaise mixture and bake for 15 to 20 minutes until the fish is cooked through. Transfer the fillets to serving plates and remove the cocktail sticks.
Add chives to the remaining sauce in the flameproof dish and cook gently on the hob for 1 to 2 minutes, whisking until smooth, pour over the fillets and serve with the potatoes or rice, green beans and lemon wedges.

Hollandaise Sauce

1 egg
2 egg yolks
juice of one lemon
$\frac{1}{2}$ teaspoon salt
225g / 8 oz butter, cut into small pieces

Put the egg yolks, lemon juice and salt into a food processor or liquidiser and blend until smooth. Gently heat the butter in a heavy based pan until completely melted and foaming. With the motor running at medium speed, pour the butter into the egg mixture through the feed tube in a continuous thin stream - the sauce will amalgamate and thicken almost immediately. Process for another 5 seconds. Pour it out of the food processor back into the hot pan. Do not return to the heat but stir gently for about 30 to 60 seconds - the heat from the pan will finish the thickening of the sauce. The sauce can be kept hot for about 10 minutes over warm water or in a switched off but warm oven.

BLUE PETER

SPICED GIRL COOKIES

225g self-raising flour
2 level teaspoons mixed spice
$\frac{1}{2}$ teaspoon ground ginger
125g light brown sugar
125g unsalted butter (softened)
1 medium egg (beaten)

Sift the flour with the spices into a mixing bowl.
Stir in the sugar and the butter (cut into small pieces).
With clean hands! - mix it altogether with your fingers until the mixture looks like breadcrumbs.
Stir in enough beaten egg to bind the mixture together and knead it into a neat ball.
Sprinkle the surface with flour.
Roll out the mixture evenly.
Cut the basic cookie shapes out using a biscuit cutter.
Put the cookies onto a lined baking tray.
Cook in a pre-heated oven at 190°C/375°F/Gas 5 for 10-15 minutes, or until golden brown.
To turn your cookies into Spiced Girl Cookies you can use coloured icing, jellied diamonds and the little gold and silver edible coloured balls.

RICHARD'S BANANA NUT CAKE

3 ripe bananas
225g Plain flour
3 teaspoons baking powder
Ground nutmeg
100g Butter
100g Soft light brown sugar
2 eggs
Optional - chopped walnuts

Sift the flour, add 3 teaspoons of baking powder and a pinch of nutmeg. Mix this and put the bowl to one side.
Take the butter and the soft brown sugar, beat together with a wooden spoon. Whisk the 2 eggs with a fork and add them to the butter and sugar mixture - a little at a time.
Beat this together and then add the 3 ripe mashed bananas. (Ripe bananas are better as they give more flavour).
Then start adding the dry ingredients (flour, baking powder and nutmeg).
If you wish to add the chopped walnuts do so at this stage.
Pour the mixture into a loaf tin which has been lined with greaseproof paper.
Place in a pre-heated oven on Gas350°F 4 or 180°C/ for 1 hour.
Check that it is cooked by prodding with a knife, if the knife comes out clean the bread is cooked.
Leave in the tin for 10 minutes and turn it out to cool.

COLORADO GIANT COOKIES

75g butter
50g white granulated sugar
100g soft brown sugar
2 Eggs
1teaspoon vanilla essence
250g plain flour
$\frac{1}{2}$ teaspoon salt
1 teaspoon bicarbonate of soda
150g chocolate chips

Cream together butter, sugar and vanilla essence until smooth.
Add the eggs and mix well.
Sift the flour with bicarbonate of soda and salt, gradually add to the mixture.
Put the mixture in the refrigerator for 20 minutes.
Pre-heat the oven to 375°F/190°C/Gas 5.
Prepare the baking tray either by greasing it or using a sheet of greaseproof paper.
Shape the mixture into small balls using a tablespoon, arrange on the baking tray (you should get about 16).
Lightly press down on each one with the ball of your hand - don't flatten them completely.
Put in the oven for 7-8 minutes.

STUART'S POTATO, CHEESE AND ONION CRUMBLE

100g cheese
1 large potato
1 onion
75g wholemeal breadcrumbs
200ml skimmed milk
dash Worcester sauce and paprika (optional)

Peel and chop the onion. Spread the onions over the bottom of an ovenproof dish and put on one side.
Grate 100g of cheese - you could use cheddar, edam, red leicester - whatever you happen to have in your fridge.
Peel, then grate the potatoes- do this carefully or you will grate your fingers! Then add the potato to the cheese.
Breadcrumbs next. These are freshly crumbled from a chunk of stale bread. Use up what you have in the cupboard - white sliced works just as well but you will find it easier to crumble if it is a day or two old.
Mix everything together with the milk and add a dash of Worcester sauce and a pinch of paprika which adds some colour.
Put in the oven on gas 6 or 200°C/400°F for 20 minutes by which time the top should have turned a lovely golden brown.
When it is cooked you could decorate the top with slices of tomato or a sprig of parsley.
Now all that is left to do is to eat it.

THE BONINGTON SALAD
SIR CHRIS BONNINGTON CBE

Can of beans (see method)
Variety of vegetables

The base is a can of beans.
These can be red kidney, butter, haricot, chick peas, flagolet or any other variety you like.
The best are ones without any sugar (obtainable from health shops).

Open and drain the can and then rinse with some water before putting the beans into a large salad bowl.
Chop and add a variety of raw vegetables.
Any combination of the following go really well:

Broccoli (full of goodness), cauliflower, mushrooms, fennel (gives it a really nice strong flavour), carrots (better finely chopped than grated), green pepper, tomato, pumpkin seeds, a sprinkling of basil and rosemary, a dollop of olive oil and a dollop of cider vinegar, some freshly ground black pepper to taste and I quite like adding some chopped garlic.

You just mix the whole lot up and have it with some wholemeal bread and margarine or butter, and some really tasty cheese.

APPLE AND RHUBARB ALMOND SPONGE
RICHARD BRANSON

Filling:
1 lb cooking apples
1 lb rhubarb
Grated rind and juice of 1 orange
3 oz demerara sugar
2 oz sultanas

Sponge:
3 oz butter
2 oz sugar
2 eggs
A few drops of almond essence
1 oz self-raising flour
1 oz ground almonds
salt
A little milk

Peel and slice apples.
Wash and cut rhubarb into 1 inch pieces.
Put into a saucepan with orange juice and rind, sugar and sultanas.
Simmer for about 15 minutes.
Pour into greased ovenproof dish.

Cream butter and sugar.
Add eggs and almond essence.
Mix in flour, ground almonds and salt.
Add a little milk to make a dropping consistency.
Then spoon over the fruit and sprinkle the top with flaked almonds.
Cook at 180°C/350°F/Gas 4 for 35-40 minutes.

Serve hot with custard or cream.

CHELSEA FOOTBALL CLUB PRE-MATCH MEAL MENU
RUUD GULLIT

Pre-Match Meal

- Grilled chicken breast
  - White rice
- Plain white pasta
- Jacket potatoes
- Selection of fresh vegetables
  - Baked beans
- Sauces - mushroom, cheese and bolognaise
  - Toast
  - Preserves
- Selection of fresh fruit

Lunch / Dinner

Please ensure fresh parmesan cheese and olive oil are available on each table

Starters

- Soup or melon

Main Course

Running buffet to include

- Grilled chicken breast
  - Grilled white fish
    - White rice
  - Plain white pasta
  - Jacket potatoes
  - Mashed potatoes
    - Baked beans
- Selection of fresh vegetables
- Sauces - mushroom, cheese and bolognaise

Drinks

- Tea, coffee, apple juice, orange juice and still mineral water

BEANS ON TOAST Á LA JEREMY
JEREMY CLARKSON

A tin of baked beans
A large dollop of butter
Tabasco sauce
2 slices of bread

Cook the beans to a near pulp on a slow heat with a large dollop of butter and six or so drops of Tabasco sauce.
Toast the bread, when cooked butter to the edges and then serve the beans mixture on the toast.

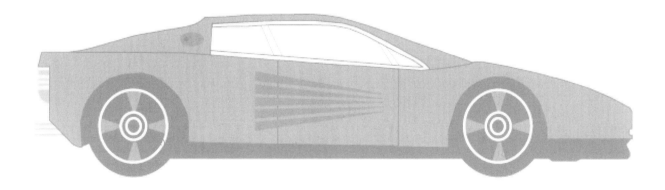

STEAK PIE
KENNY DALGLISH

Serves 4

1x15 ml spoon (1tablespoon) oil
675g (1½lb) braising steak, cubed
675g (1½lb) onion sliced
450ml (¾pt) cold water
3x15ml (3tbsp) Bisto onion gravy granules
1 bay leaf
1½x 5ml spoon (1½ teaspoon.) oregano
250g (9oz) ready made puff pastry

Heat the oil in a large saucepan and fry the meat until sealed and brown on all sides.
Remove from the pan.
Fry the onions until soft and return the meat to the pan.
Pour the cold water over the meat and onions, sprinkle in the gravy granules, bring to the boil stirring all the time. Stir in the bay leaf and oregano. Reduce the heat, cover and simmer, stirring occasionally, for 1½ hours until the meat is tender. Remove the bay leaf and transfer the meat and onions to a 1.1 litre (2 pint) pie dish with enough gravy to fill half the pie dish.
Heat the oven to 220°C/425°F/Gas 7. Roll out the pastry larger than the pie dish. Cut off 1cm (½ in) strip of pastry. Dampen the edges of the dish. Place pastry strip around the edge and damp again. Cover the dish with pastry, seal the edges firmly and trim off any excess pastry. Decorate with pastry leaves, make a small hole in the centre and brush with milk.
Bake in the oven for 10-15 minutes then reduce the heat to 190°C/375°F/Gas 5 for a further 15-20 minutes until pastry is golden brown and the filling thoroughly heated.

CHICKEN IN WHITE WINE AND MUSHROOM SAUCE
TONY DOBBIN

2 chicken breasts
Ready-made white wine and mushroom sauce !
Jersey potatoes
Broccoli

Cook chicken fillets on 200°C/400°F/Gas 6 for 40 mins until golden brown.

Heat up sauce in pan for 5 mins.

Boil Jersey potatoes and broccoli.

Place chicken on plate, pour sauce over and serve with new potatoes and Broccoli.

BETTY'S HOTPOT
BETTY DRIVER

1 lb (450g) scragend or best end neck of lamb chopped
1½ lbs (675g) potatoes, peeled
1 large onion
Salt and pepper

½ - ¾ pint (290 - 425 ml) chicken stock
1 oz lard or dripping

Pre-heat the oven to 190°C/375°F/Gas 5

Fry the meat quickly to give it a good brown colour.
Put the meat into a casserole dish.
Slice the peeled potatoes and onions thinly.
Arrange them on top of the meat, seasoning them as you go along, overlap the top layers of potatoes.
Pour in the stock
Melt the lard and brush over the top of the potatoes.
Cover the dish and bake in the oven for at least 2 hours.
Uncover the dish and turn the oven up until the top browns.

Serve with pickled cabbage, beetroot or chutney.

PENNE DI ADAMO
KAREN DRURY

1 finely chopped onion
1 clove garlic
1 tin tomatoes
1 dried chilli
Pinch of sugar
2 tablespoons mascarpone cheese
Vodka
Pasta

Soften onion and clove of garlic in olive oil (slowly).
Add tin of tomatoes and dried chilli and slowly again allow to thicken, adding a pinch of sugar.
When sauce is thick add 2 tablespoons of mascarpone cheese, take off the heat and add enough Vodka to thin the sauce to a coating consistency.
Add to ' al dente ' pasta - the sauce should lightly cover all the pasta.
Eat immediately.

VEGETABLE CRUMBLE
MARY DUFF

Serves 4

1 cauliflower broken into florets
Salt to taste
2 tablespoons oil
4 tablespoons whole-wheat flour
350ml (12floz) milk
1x326g (11½oz) can sweetcorn (drained)
2 tablespoons chopped parsley
125g (4oz) mature cheddar cheese grated

Topping

50g(2oz) whole-wheat flour
25g(1oz) margarine
25g (1oz) porridge oats
25g (1oz) chopped almonds

Cook the cauliflower in boiling salted water for 5 minutes. Drain, reserving the water.
Heat the oil in the same pan and stir in the flour. Remove from the heat, add the milk, stirring until blended. Add ¼ of the reserved cooking liquid, bring to the boil and cook for 3 minutes until thickened. Stir in the sweetcorn, parsley and half the cheese.
Gently fold in the cauliflower and turn into a 1.5 litre (3 pint) ovenproof dish.

For the topping, place the flour in a bowl and rub in the margarine until the mixture resembles fine breadcrumbs. Add the remaining cheese. Sprinkle over the vegetable mixture and bake in a preheated oven 190°C/375°F/Gas 5 for 30 minutes until golden brown and crisp.

ITALIAN PASTA
JONATHAN EDWARDS

Serves 2 - 3

10 oz spaghetti or pasta shapes
8 oz bacon
14 oz can tinned chopped tomatoes
6 oz mushrooms
Herbs
Salt and pepper
6 oz cheddar cheese
1 pint milk
Cornflour

Cook the pasta in boiling salted water for approximately 12-15 minutes or until tender.

Meanwhile chop the bacon and mushrooms and dry fry, add the chopped tomatoes and herbs, simmer until the bacon and mushrooms are tender.

Pour almost the whole pint of milk into a pan and bring to the boil. Mix the remainder of the milk with the cornflour, when the milk boils thicken with the cornflour mix, remove from the heat. Add grated cheese and salt/pepper to taste, stir thoroughly.

Now mix the drained pasta with the bacon mix and the cheese sauce in an ovenproof dish. (Place the dish on a baking tray in case the sauce boils over). Sprinkle the top with grated cheese and bake on 190°C/375°F/Gas 4-5 until piping hot, the top is crispy and the dishes are washed!

BEANS ON TOAST WITH BEER AND TELLY
BEN ELTON

Make toast (must be white sliced)
Butter (must be butter)
Heat beans (preferably Heinz)
Pour beans onto toast, open beer, turn on telly.

GRILLED SEA BASS WITH FETTUCINI AND RATATOUILLE SAUCE
ALEX FERGUSON

Main Dish

Serves 4
450g (1lb) pasta dough
50g (2oz) unsalted butter
salt and freshly ground black pepper
4 sea bass fillets each about175-225g (6-8oz)
25ml (1floz) olive oil

For the Ratatouille sauce

1 red pepper seeded
1 green pepper seeded
2 shallots
Half an aubergine
25g (1oz) unsalted butter
25g (1floz) olive oil
300ml (10floz) red pepper coulis
1 courgette

To make the fettuccini, roll the dough through a pasta machine several times until it becomes about 1mm (1/16in) thick, then pass it through the noodle cutter and leave to rest. If you do not have a pasta machine, it can be divided, rolled several times until very thin, then cut by hand into ribbons; a pizza wheel is the easiest way to cut pasta.

Pre-heat the grill to medium; add butter and season a flameproof baking tray.

To make the ratatouille, cut the vegetables into 5mm (1/4in) dice. Melt the butter with the olive oil in a large pan. Add the diced vegetables and cook for about 3-4 minutes until just softened. In another pan, warm the red pepper coulis then add the vegetables. Season with salt and pepper.

Lay the sea bass fillets on the prepared tray skin side up and cook under the medium grill for about 8 minutes.

While the fish is cooking, boil a large pan of water with the olive oil and a good pinch of salt. When boiling drop in the pasta and move it around with a fork. If it is fresh, it will only take a few minutes to cook. For dried pasta just follow the instructions on the packet. Drain through a colander, season with salt and pepper and toss with the remaining butter to loosen.

Warm the ratatouille sauce and spoon it on to hot plates. Sit the fettuccini in the middle and lay the sea bass on the top.

JO MANAZATTI
MICHAEL FISH

Serves 10

2lb lean pork fillet cut into small pieces
8 onions, chopped
1 large jar tomato puree and 2 cups water
$^3/_4$ lb mushrooms sliced
1 tin creamed mushrooms or condensed
mushroom soup
2 green peppers
1lb strong cheddar cheese cubed
Salt, pepper and cayenne
1oz margarine
1 packet shell noodles
Cheese to grate on top

Melt the margarine, brown the onions and pork and put into a large mixing bowl.
Add all the other ingredients, except the noodles.
Boil the noodles for 15 minutes, strain well and add to the mixture.
Put in a large ovenproof casserole dish, grate some cheese on top and put the lid on.
Put into a preheated oven 350°F/180°C/Gas 4 for one hour.

This is delicious served with a tossed green salad and garlic bread.

SPICY BEANS WITH MASH
JEROME FLYNN

Serves 4

1 can of fusilaye beans (or cannellini)
1 can chick peas
3 tablespoons olive oil
1 large onion
Fresh coriander and parsley (chopped)
1 tube tomato puree
4/5 cloves garlic
Fresh lemon juice
Salt and pepper to taste
Chilli sauce if desired

Fry the onions gently in the oil until softened, stirring in some parsley. Add the beans and chickpeas with their juice followed by the crushed garlic. If you like it very tomatoey, mix the whole tube of puree with a dash of water in a jug and add to the pan along with salt and pepper. The chilli sauce is optional, just add as much as you want.

Cook everything gently for 15-20 minutes then add freshly squeezed juice of at least half a lemon together with a generous sprinkling of coriander leaves. Cover and cook for a further 5-10 minutes, then serve with mashed potatoes and peas.

This dish is also wonderful with buckwheat or cous cous instead of spuds and is how the Turkish would have originally eaten it. My final tip is to mix some live yoghurt laced with mint and chopped cucumber to put on the side as a delicious cooling accompaniment.

BEEF WELLINGTON
DAVID GOWER

Serves 6 - 8

3 lbs beef fillet
$1/4$ lb paté
$1/2$ lb finely chopped mushrooms
1 lb puff pastry (or shortcrust)
Beaten egg to glaze
Salt
Pepper
1 tablespoon oil

Pre-heat oven to 230°C/425°F/Gas 7. Rub the beef with salt, pepper and oil. Roast on a rack for 40 minutes. Remove and leave to cool.

When cool, cover the top and sides with the paté and chopped mushrooms.

Roll out the pastry to $1/4$ in thickness - large enough to envelope the meat.
Put the fillet top side down on the pastry, and enclose into a parcel sealing the ends.
Turn meat seam side down and decorate with spare pastry if you can be bothered!
Glaze with the beaten egg.

Bake for a further 40 minutes or so, till the pastry is golden brown and puffed up.

Tastes even better if served with a red wine sauce.

CHEESE BAKED POTATO WITH SALAD
ANGELA GRIFFIN

Take a large potato and place in the microwave for 6 minutes.

Take a lettuce, cucumber, tomato, celery, spring onion, red onion and chop it all up.

Take the potato and place in the middle of a plate, chop some cheese and put in the potato, put in the microwave and cook for 1 minute.

Place the salad on the plate around the potato.

Slice mozzarella cheese and feta cheese, put on top of salad.

Put philidelphia and butter in the potato, add lots of Italian dressing to the salad.

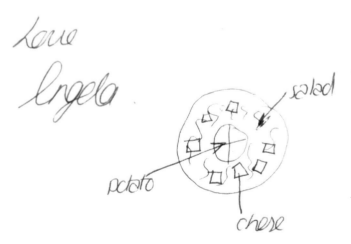

ESMAY'S PUDDING
LORD INGLEWOOD

1 oz butter
4 oz caster sugar
2 oz self-raising flour
Juice of 2 lemons
Grated rind of 1 lemon
1½ cups of milk
2 eggs

Cream together 1 oz butter and 4 oz caster sugar.
Add 2 oz sifted self-raising flour.
Mix.
Add juice of 2 lemons and grated rind of 1.
Then add 1½ cups of milk and 2 beaten egg yolks.
Lastly add the 2 stiffly whipped egg whites.
Pour into a lightly buttered baking dish.
Stand the dish in a tin of hot water to come half-way up the side and bake 180°C/350°F/Gas 4s for about 45 minutes, until golden brown.

Serve hot with cream.

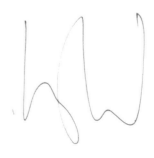

EAMONN HOLMES MUM'S HOME COOKING RECIPES
APPLE CAKES

3 cups of plain flour
6 oz margarine
$\frac{1}{2}$ teaspoon salt
Water to bind
$\frac{1}{2}$ lb. apples sliced

Peel apples - you can either cook to taste or put on rolled pastry raw.
Sprinkle lightly with sugar and put top layer of pastry over apples.
When cooked add another sprinkle of sugar to cake.

Cook in oven on 180°C/350°F/Gas 4 for 30 minutes.

FAIRY CAKES

6 oz self-raising flour
6 oz caster sugar
3 eggs
1 teaspoon baking powder
1 tablespoon tepid water
Smidgen vanilla essence

Mix ingredients together, spoon into paper cases and cook in the oven on electric 180°C/350°F/Gas 4 for 15 minutes.

(Approximately 24 cakes)

SOUP / BROTH

Eamonn's mum uses his favourite which is steak end but any meat could be used.

Add water to a packet of soup mixture and immerse meat - bring to the boil and simmer for 1 $\frac{1}{2}$ hours (or until meat is tender)

Remove meat and add celery, parsley, leeks, one beef stock cube and simmer for 10 minutes.
Can be cooked in the oven or on top.

MUM'S STEW

Cut potatoes small and cover with water adding onion, carrots. oxo cubes and mince steak.

Bring to boil and simmer for $\frac{1}{2}$ hour.

A little secret - Eamonn likes a little sprinkle of curry powder added to his stew when served.

CHAMP

Salted boiled potatoes
Chop spring onions and put in a saucepan with a small amount of boiling milk for 5 minutes.
Mash together and serve with a big lump of butter.

Mum says it's best served with tasty codfish and goes down particularly well with a glass of buttermilk.

HOT CARPACCIO WITH SALSA VERDE
Sarah Kennedy

150g beef fillet
25 ml olive oil
2 teaspoons dark soy sauce
Black pepper

For the Salsa Verde:

3 anchovy fillets, drained
2 cloves garlic, crushed
$\frac{1}{2}$ teaspoon Balsamic vinegar
1 teaspoon capers, roughly chopped
1 teaspoon Fresh parsley, chopped
50 ml olive oil

With a sharp knife, cut the beef into four 5mm slices. Place each slice between 2 sheets of dampened greaseproof paper and flatten them by beating with a meat mallet or rolling pin until they have doubled the size and are almost transparent. Be careful not to tear the meat. Lay the slices in a shallow, non-metallic dish. Whisk together the olive oil and soy sauce and season with plenty of black pepper. Pour over the meat, cover and leave to marinate for up to 12 hours. Pre-heat oven to Gas 9/240°C/475°F.

For the salsa verde, pound the anchovies in a pestle and mortar or in a strong bowl with the end of a rolling pin. Stir in the crushed garlic and the balsamic vinegar. Add the chopped capers and parsley and gradually mix in the olive oil. Season with black pepper. It should not be necessary to add salt as the anchovies are quite salty. Lay the meat in a single layer on two baking sheets and place in the oven for 2 minutes. Transfer to 2 warmed serving plates and serve immediately, dressed with the salsa verde.
Serve accompanied by pasta with courgette and carrot ribbons and French beans with feta cheese and sundried tomatoes.

PARTRIDGE WITH GARLIC AND KUMQUATS
MICHAEL KNIGHTON

CARLISLE
UNITED

3 Partridge each weight about 700g (1½ lb) (Poussin or Quail could be substituted, or 1 Pheasant or Guinea Fowl.)
Sea salt & freshly ground black pepper
225g (8 oz) fresh kumquats
16 garlic cloves (or adjust to taste)
30 ml (2 tbsp) olive oil
25g (1 oz) unsalted butter
2 bay leaves
450 ml (¾ pint) dry cider or use "Scrumpy"
200 ml (7 fl oz) apple juice
200 ml (7 fl oz) double cream
Fresh thyme or coriander to garnish

Cut both sides of the backbone of the partridge with a pair of poultry or kitchen scissors and remove. Cut the partridge in half along the breastbone. (If using pheasant or guinea fowl, you may need to adjust this method to suit.) Season the skin of the partridge or poultry with plenty of sea salt, this makes it crisp and golden. Sprinkle the skin side liberally with 10 ml (2 level tsp.) salt. Halve the kumquats. Cook the whole, unpeeled garlic cloves in a pan of boiling salted water for 4 minutes, drain, cool slightly and peel. (Or alternatively crush on a board with a kitchen knife.)

Heat the oil in a shallow, flameproof casserole (this should be large enough for the partridge halves to fit in a single layer.) If not, use a large frying pan to brown the partridge, then transfer to a casserole. Add the butter. When the butter begins to sizzle, add the partridge halves skin side down and cook for 4-5 minutes, or until deep golden brown. Remove the partridge. Add the kumquats and garlic cloves and stir over the heat for 2-3 minutes, or until golden. Return the partridge to the casserole dish, add the bay leaves and coriander and cover.

Cook at 200°C/400°F/Gas 6, for 30-35 minutes, until the partridge are cooked through. With a slotted spoon, lift the partridge, kumquats and the six garlic cloves onto a baking sheet. Cover with foil and keep warm in the oven.

With a wooden spoon, crush the remaining garlic cloves in the casserole to a paste. Add the cider and apple juice, bring to the boil and bubble for 7-10 minutes, or until syrupy. Pour in the cream (for a less rich sauce, use 142 ml (5 fl oz) carton of double cream). Season and bring back to the boil. Simmer for 1 minute. Return the partridge, whole garlic and kumquats to the casserole, cover and cook gently for 2-3 minutes.

Garnish the partridge with sprigs of thyme and coriander and serve with Spinach Mash.

SPINACH MASH
MICHAEL KNIGHTON

Preparation time: 5 minutes
Cooking time: 30 minutes

1.4 kg (3 lb) old potatoes
Freshly ground sea salt and milled black pepper
50g (2 oz) unsalted butter
100 ml (4 fl oz) milk
350g (12 oz) washed and prepared fresh medium spinach
Freshly ground nutmeg

Cut the potatoes into even sized pieces and cook in boiling, salted water for about 30 minutes, until tender. Drain well. Return the potatoes to the pan and mash them over a low heat. Add the butter.

In a large saucepan, heat the milk until just boiling. Add the spinach and stir until just wilted, (or alternatively cook in a ceramic bowl in a microwave for 3 minutes.)

Beat the spinach and milk into the potatoes. Season well with salt, pepper and grated nutmeg before serving.

FIGS, DAMSONS OR APRICOTS IN CINNAMON SYRUP
MICHAEL KNIGHTON

Preparation time: 15 minutes
Cooking time: 35 minutes (plus cooking and chilling)
Calories per serving: 370 approximately (high fibre)

1 orange
1 lemon
300 ml ($\frac{1}{2}$ pint) red wine
50g (2 oz) caster sugar
1 cinnamon stick
450g (1lb) ready to eat fresh figs or use dried figs, or fresh damsons or apricots
200g tub Mascarpone cheese or natural yoghurt

Pare the rind from the orange and lemon and place in a medium saucepan. Squeeze and add the orange and lemon juice with the wine, sugar and cinnamon stick. Bring very slowly to the boil, stirring occasionally.

Add the figs or damsons. Simmer very gently for 20 minutes until plump and soft.

Remove figs, rind and cinnamon with a slotted spoon, transfer to a serving bowl.

Return the liquid to the boil and bubble until syrupy (about 5 minutes). Pour over the figs or damsons, then cool, cover and refrigerate.

If wished, warm figs or damsons in the syrup for 3-4 minutes, then serve with mascarpone or natural yoghurt.

This dish can be kept covered in the fridge for up to one week. Just stir occasionally.

STEAK NORMANDY
JOHN LAWRENCE

Serves 4

1lb stewing steak
2 onions
2 tablespoons vinegar
2 tablespoons tomato puree
$\frac{1}{2}$ pt stock
1 tablespoon sugar
4 rashers bacon
Clove garlic
Salt and pepper

Chop the onions and the garlic and fry in some oil for several minutes.
Add the stewing steak and cook until brown.
Then add the tomato puree, vinegar and sugar.
Stir in the stock and bring to the boil.
Add seasoning.

Place everything in a casserole dish and cover with the rashers of bacon.
Cover and cook in the oven at 200°C/400°F/Gas 6 for about 2 hours.

John Lawrence

FOOL PROOF PAVLOVA
THE RIGHT HON. DAVID MACLEAN MP

Serves 8

4 egg whites
8 oz caster sugar
1 teaspoon vanilla essence
1 teaspoon vinegar
2 teaspoons cornflour
Cream to fill (approx. 15 fl oz)
Choice of fruit as preferred - strawberries, mango, peaches etc.

Pre-heat the oven to 150°C/300°F/Gas 2
Mark a 9 inch circle on a greaseproof sheet. Lightly oil the paper.
Whisk the egg whites in a large basin until stiff. Continue whisking, adding sugar a tablespoon at a time until the mixture is thick and glossy and all sugar is used up.

Fold in the vanilla essence, vinegar and cornflour. Sprinkle them well over mixture so they don't all clot in one place. (Folding sounds difficult, but if you stir in a figure of 8 it mixes well and anyway you cannot really do any harm to this mixture).

Either spoon mixture inside the marked circle (or pipe with a big cream nozzle) into a pretty shape with a well in the middle and the outside edge slightly higher.

Bake in a pre-heated oven for 1 hour. Cool and transfer to a serving plate. If possible turn off the oven and let it cool inside the oven. Better still is to make the Pavlova the night before and let it cool in the oven overnight. Some cracking is inevitable, it does not matter.

Decorate with cream and fruit. Pavlova always looks and tastes impressive (no matter how mediocre a cook one is) the middle is marshmallowy and it is usually the first choice of all desserts.

MEXICAN CHICKEN
Norma Major

8 chicken thighs
75g flour
1 teaspoon paprika
1 teaspoon salt
$\frac{1}{4}$ teaspoon ground black pepper
50g butter
30ml oil
1 onion
45ml lemon juice
30ml Worcester sauce
30ml Tabasco sauce
300ml water
150ml tomato ketchup
1 teaspoon sugar
1 teaspoon chilli powder
$\frac{1}{4}$ teaspoon oregano

Shake chicken in flour, salt, paprika and black pepper.
Brown chicken in foaming butter and oil, place in baking dish.
Add onion to oil and butter and cook until soft.
Add all remaining ingredients and cook for 10 minutes over gentle heat.
Pour mixture over chicken; cover and bake until tender, keeping well basted.

Serve with rice and green salad.

AUBERGINE GOAT CHEESE SAVOURY CUSTARD
MILLER HOWE

Serves 4

Lightly butter four ramekins

2 tablespoons olive oil
4 oz finely chopped onions
4 oz finely chopped red peppers
8 thin slices aubergine (cut to fit ramekins, leaving about $1/8$ in round the side)
that have been laid out on kitchen paper and lightly sprinkled with salt and left for an hour.
4 x $1/4$ inch circles of your favourite goats cheese
$1/4$ pint double cream
1 medium egg
1 medium egg yolk
half nutmeg finely grated

Fry off the onions and red peppers until golden - leave to cool.
Place one circle of aubergine in each ramekin and on top of this put an eighth of the onion and pepper mix.
On top of this put the cheese followed by the pepper and onion mix finishing off with the aubergine slice.
Lightly beat the cream eggs and nutmeg and divide between the four ramekins.
Preheat oven to 185°C/375°F/Gas 5 place your ramekins in a small roasting tray and pour boiling water half way up their sides.
Cook for 30 mins.

Leave for 10 mins to cool and then run a sharp knife around the edge and turn out.
Serve with tomato sauce.

AVOCADO ON TOAST
MYSTIC MEG

Take a ripe avocado, mash with a dash of lemon juice and freshly ground black pepper, then spread on thick slices of hot brown toast.

40

Thai Chicken
JOHN NELLIST

4 boneless chicken breasts
2oz. coconut cream
5 fluid ounces chicken stock
1 tablespoon sunflower oil
1 green chilli, sliced
4 spring onions, chopped
2 tablespoons peanut butter
finely grated rind and juice of one lime
small bunch of coriander or parsley

Cut chicken into long thin strips.
Dissolve coconut cream in the chicken stock.

Heat the oil in a wok or large heavy pan and fry the chicken, stirring until golden.
Stir in the chilli and onions, and cook gently for a few minutes.
Stir in the coconut cream, peanut butter, lime rind and juice, and simmer, uncovered, stirring for about 8 - 10 minutes.

Scatter with coriander or parsley and serve with boiled rice and green salad or seasonal vegetables.
This dish is extremely simple to make, but the lovely blend of flavours makes it quite special.

CHICKEN KORMA WITH CORIANDER LEAVES
PATSY PALMER

1kg chicken	5 garlic cloves
10- 12 strands saffron	2 onions, chopped
5 green chillies, chopped	1 cup full fat yoghurt
$\frac{1}{4}$ cup of ghee or oil	4 cloves
8 green cardamoms	4in (10cm) cinnamon stick
$\frac{1}{2}$ teaspoon ginger powder	Salt
2 cups chicken stock	$\frac{1}{4}$ teaspoon ground pepper
2 tablespoons chopped coriander leaves	$\frac{1}{2}$ teaspoon turmeric powder

Boil the chicken in 3 cups of water along with 2 of the garlic cloves for 3-4 minutes. Strain and discard water. Leave the chicken to cool, then rinse in lukewarm water. This removes all the odour of the chicken. Cut up the chicken.

Pound the remaining garlic and soak in $\frac{1}{2}$ cup of water to obtain a garlic infusion. Soak the saffron strands in $\frac{1}{4}$ cup water, pressing with the back of a spoon to get an infusion. Puree the onions with green chillies. Whisk the yoghurt and set aside.

Heat the ghee or oil in a cooking pot and fry the onion puree until golden (about 12 - 15 minutes). Add the cloves, cardamoms and cinnamon followed by the turmeric powder. Add the chicken, garlic infusion and yoghurt and cover with a lid. Allow to simmer for 7 - 10 minutes until the juices are absorbed.

Add the ginger powder and salt to taste and sauté for 3-4 minutes until the chicken is lightly browned. Add enough chicken stock to get the amount of gravy desired (this dish does not need a great deal)

Simmer for 40 minutes over a gentle heat. When the chicken is tender, sprinkle with the saffron infusion, pepper and fresh coriander leaves.

HILARY'S GRANDMOTHER'S RECIPE FOR CHOPPED LIVER
ESTHER RANTZEN

2 lbs chicken liver
1 large spanish onion
3-4 hard boiled eggs
1 tablespoon melted chicken fat (optional)
Oil for frying onions and liver
Salt and pepper to taste

Fry the sliced onion in a little oil until golden (for about 10 minutes). Remove from the pan. Chop in food processor for about 1 minute until very finely chopped. Place in a bowl.

Fry the livers until well done (about 10 minutes). Chop in food processor until smooth. Add to the onions.

Reserve one egg yolk for garnish. Finely chop hard boiled eggs in food processor. Add to liver and onions and mix to smooth pate. If it is not moist enough a little of the pan juices may be added or about one tablespoon of chicken fat. Season to taste with salt and pepper. Garnish with chopped egg yolk.

That's Life

PORK PUDDING
ERIC ROBSON

1 lb. flour
¾ lb diced pork (cooked and skinned belly pork will do)
¾ lb seedless raisins
1 egg
Some milk
Salt and freshly ground black pepper to season the mixture

Mix all the ingredients together until they're the consistency of a stiff batter, pour into a greased baking tin and cook in a moderate oven until well cooked. Allow to cool, slice and serve with mixed pickles.

DUTCH POTATO BROCCOLI
ANITA RODDICK OBE

Overall timing: 1 hour   -   Serves 4-6

3 large boiling potatoes, peeled, diced
375ml cream
125ml water
15ml cornflour
500ml chopped fresh broccoli
125ml smooth peanut butter
1 onion
Parmesan cheese

Cook potatoes in cream and water
Do not drain, thicken with cornflour mixed with a small amount of water.
Meanwhile, chop broccoli into ¹/₂in chunks and cook until fork tender.
Add to potato mixture, along with peanut butter and onion.
Stir well to mix.
Put into a buttered 3-litre casserole and sprinkle generously with parmesan cheese.
Bake at 350°F/180°C/Gas 4 for 30 minutes.

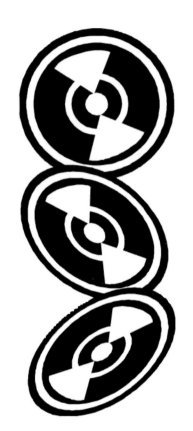

SINGLE MAN'S LUNCH
SIR JAMES SAVILE

One can soup
One can beans

Pour into a dish.
Heat in the microwave.
Eat.

POTATO CAKES
PHILLIP SCHOFIELD

Potatoes
Milk
Butter
Salt
Self-raising Flour

Peel and boil sufficient potatoes needed for the amount of people.

When cooked, mash in the usual way with lots of milk and butter

Add salt to taste.

Add enough self-raising flour to make a stiff dough. Roll out on a floured board into individual circles about 5in across and $\frac{1}{2}$in deep.

Cook near the top of a hot oven for about 15-20 mins until golden brown.
Butter and eat immediately.

SHARROW BREAD & BUTTER PUDDING

$\frac{1}{2}$ pint of double cream
$\frac{1}{2}$ pint milk
3 eggs
vanilla pod
A little salt
3oz caster sugar
3 Small bread rolls or 8 slices of white bread with crusts removed
Butter for spreading
$\frac{1}{2}$oz Sultanas, soaked in a little rum
$\frac{1}{2}$oz mixed peel

Serves 4

Bring milk, cream, and vanilla pod to the boil

Lightly mix eggs and sugar together

Add simmering milk and cream

Pass through a sieve

Arrange buttered bread in an ovenproof dish. Add sultanas and mixed
Finish with a layer of bread. Pour mixture over and allow to soak.

Place in a bain-marie and cook for 35-45 minutes

Sprinkle with apricot jam and dust with icing sugar

Serve with double cream or apricot sauce or both.

Sharrow Bay Hotel

48

SPAGHETTI BOLOGNESE
ALAN SHEARER

6 tablespoons of olive or sunflower oil
1 finely chopped onion
1 finely chopped carrot
2 sticks of finely chopped celery
1 clove of garlic, crushed
2 oz streaky bacon, finely chopped
1 lb lean minced beef
¼ pint of red wine
3 tablespoons tomato puree
14 oz can of chopped tomatoes
Salt and pepper
Pinch of sugar
2 bay leaves

Heat oil in a large saucepan and fry the onion, carrot, celery and garlic until soft.
Stir in bacon and fry for a further 5 minutes.
Mix in beef and brown, stirring all the time.
Pour in the wine and bring to the boil.
Stir in the tomato puré, tomatoes and seasoning.
Cover and simmer for 2 hours.

Cook spaghetti as directed.

ROASTED MEDITERRANEAN VEGETABLE LASAGNE
DELIA SMITH

Serves 4-6

Approx. 9 sheets spinach lasagne (the kind that needs no pre-cooking)

For the Filling:
1 lb (450g) cherry tomatoes, skinned
1 small aubergine
2 medium courgettes
1 small red pepper, de-seeded and cut into 1 inch (2.5 cm) squares
1 small yellow pepper, de-seeded and cut into 1 inch (2.5 cm) squares
1 large onion, sliced and cut into 1 inch (2.5 cm) squares
2 fat cloves garlic, crushed
3 tablespoons extra virgin olive oil
2 oz (50g) pitted black olives, chopped
1 heaped tablespoon capers, drained
2 tablespoons fresh basil, leaves torn so that they stay quite visible
3 oz (75g) mozzarella cheese, grated
salt and freshly milled black pepper

For the Sauce:
$1\frac{1}{4}$ oz (35g) plain flour
$1\frac{1}{2}$ oz (40g) butter
1 pint (570ml) milk
1 bayleaf
a grating of fresh nutmeg
salt and freshly milled black pepper
3 tablespoons grated Reggio Parmesan cheese

For the Topping:
1 tablespoon grated Reggio Parmesan cheese

You will also need a large, shallow roasting-tin (or rimmed oven shelf) and a heatproof baking-dish measuring 9 x 9 inches x 2 inches deep (25 x 25 cm x 5 cm deep).

Pre-heat the oven to Gas 9/475°F/240°C

Prepare the aubergine and courgettes ahead of time by cutting them into 1 inch (2.5 cm) dice, leaving the skins on. Then toss the dice in about a level dessertspoon of salt and pack them into a colander with a plate on top and a heavy weight on top of the plate. Leave them on one side for an hour so that some of the bitter juices drain out. After that squeeze out any juices left, and dry the dice thoroughly in a clean cloth.

Now arrange the tomatoes, aubergine, courgettes, peppers and onion in the roasting-tin, sprinkle with the chopped garlic, basil and olive oil, toss everything around in the oil to get a good coating, and season with salt and pepper. Now place the tin on the highest shelf of the oven for 30-40 minutes or until the vegetables are toasted brown at the edges.

Meanwhile, make the sauce by placing all the ingredients (except the cheese) in a small saucepan and whisking continuously over a medium heat until the sauce boils and thickens. Then turn the heat down to its lowest and let the sauce cook for 2 minutes. Now add the grated Parmesan. When the vegetables are done, remove them from the oven and stir in the chopped olives and the capers. Turn the oven down to Gas 4/350°F/180°C.

Now, into the baking-dish pour one quarter of the sauce, followed by one third of the vegetable mixture. Then sprinkle in a third of the mozzarella and follow this with a single layer of lasagne sheets. Repeat this process, ending up with a final layer of sauce and a good sprinkling of grated Parmesan. Now place the dish in the oven and bake for 25-30 minutes or until the top is crusty and golden. All this needs is a plain lettuce salad with a lemony dressing as an accompaniment.

HADDOCK & EGG MORNAY
BILL TARMEY

Serves 4

4 smoked haddock fillets
1 bouquet garni
³/₄ pt/450ml milk
1 ¹/₂oz /40g butter
1 ¹/₂oz /40g flour
3oz/75g grated cheese
Salt and pepper
4 eggs
Parsley to garnish

Cook the fish with a little milk and the bouquet garni for 10 minutes.
Drain the fish and place in a buttered ovenproof dish.
Keep the fish warm. Poach the eggs in a little water in a pan.
Melt the butter, stir in the flour, gradually stir in the milk.
Bring to the boil, stirring continuously until thickened.
Add 2oz/50g grated cheese, salt and pepper. Place the eggs over the
haddock fillets and pour over the cheese sauce.
Sprinkle with the remaining cheese.
Place under the grill for 4-5 minutes until lightly browned.
Garnish with parsley.

MRS BELL'S MOUSSAKA
ALAN TITCHMARSH

1lb mince
$^{1}/_{2}$ lb spaghetti
1 pint cheese Sauce
1 onion
Garlic
Handful sultanas
$^{1}/_{2}$ teaspoon mixed herbs
Nutmeg
1 tablespoon brown sugar
Small tin tomatoes
(glass of red wine optional)

Fry mince with all above, except cheese sauce and spaghetti.
Thicken with flour.
Moisten with stock or water, but leave quite firm.
Put in a deep pie dish
Boil the spaghetti
Make a thick white sauce and grate cheese into it.
To each $^{1}/_{2}$ pint of sauce add 1 desert spoonful of vinegar with cheese.
Put the boiled spaghetti on the mince.
Pour over the cheese sauce.
Cook for 30 mins. Gas 4/350˚F/180˚C

CARLINS
ERIC WALLACE

Soak a pan of carlins overnight, rinse them, put them in a pan with water about quarter of an inch higher than the carlins. Add salt, pepper, vinegar to taste and a teaspoonfull of sugar. Simmer for about half an hour (keep an eye on it to make sure the carlins don't go dry) then serve with a big blob of butter.

COCKLES
JULIE WALTERS

$1/4$ pt Fresh cockles
2 slices of Wholemeal bread
Butter
Freshly ground pepper

Butter bread, place cockles on one piece, sprinkle with pepper, cover with the other piece, open mouth, shove in, clamp teeth down on bread and masticate.

WHICKER'S WORLDly FISH PIE
ALAN WHICKER

2 lbs mixed fish (cod, smoked haddock, whiting or any white fish)
$\frac{1}{4}$ lb prawns
4 oz butter
2 oz flour
1 pint of milk
2 hardboiled eggs, chopped
1 tablespoon capers
3 tablespoons parsley
1 tablespoon lemon juice
Salt and pepper

Topping:
2 lb potatoes
1 oz butter
1 carton sour cream
Nutmeg

Arrange fish in a buttered baking tin, season and pour over half a pint of milk.
Dot with butter and bake for 15-20 minutes.
Reserve liquid.
Flake fish into large pieces.
Make a white sauce with butter, flour, half a pint of milk and the liquid you have reserved, adding extra milk if required.
Put fish into sauce with prawns, egg, capers, parsley, salt and pepper.
Stir in lemon juice.
Place in buttered baking dish.
Mash potatoes and blend with sour cream. Add salt and pepper to taste and a good grating of nutmeg.
Cover fish with the potato mixture and bake for half an hour.
Oven temperature - 200°C/400°F/Gas 6

FRUIT CHEESECAKE
RUBY WAX

For the Crust

1$\frac{1}{2}$ cups finely crushed ginger biscuits
$\frac{1}{4}$ cup castor sugar
6 tablespoons melted butter
1 teaspoon cinnamon

For the Filling

2$\frac{1}{2}$ cups canned cubed pineapple
2 tablespoons gelatin
3 egg yolks
$\frac{1}{2}$ cup sugar
$\frac{1}{2}$ cup pineapple juice
1lb smooth cottage cheese
1 teaspoon grated lemon rind
3 tablespoons lemon juice
$\frac{1}{4}$ teaspoon salt
2 cups whipped cream
3 stiffly beaten egg whites
a pinch of cinnamon

To make the crust, finely crush the biscuits, then stir in the rest of the crust ingredients and mix well together. Pat the mixture into a 10" pie dish and chill thoroughly in the fridge.

To make the filling, drain the canned pineapple, reserving the juice. Soak the gelatin in $\frac{1}{2}$ cup of the reserved juice. Meanwhile, lightly beat the egg yolks and stir in the sugar and $\frac{1}{2}$ cup of pineapple juice.

Cook these ingredients in a double boiler over a pan of hot water, stirring constantly, until they thicken. Add the soaked gelatin and stir until dissolved. Leave the custard to cool. When it is cooled, stir in the cottage cheese, lemon rind, lemon juice and the salt. Then stir in $3/4$ of the pineapple cubes and 2 cups of whipped cream. Then fold in the egg whites. Pour this mixture into the piecrust and decorate the top with the rest of the pineapple cubes and a sprinkling of cinnamon. Chill in the fridge for at least 3 hours.

SALAD DRESSING
VISCOUNT WHITELAW

Mix together:
8 teaspoons caster sugar
8 level teaspoons mustard
2 teaspoons salt
A good sprinkling of black pepper

In a second bowl mix together:
16 tablespoons Salad oil
8 dessertspoons Vinegar

Pour a small amount of the second mixture into the first and mix.
Add the rest and mix thoroughly.

Viscount Whitelaw

CHICKEN LIVER PATE
BARBARA WINDSOR

2 pots of frozen chicken livers
6 oz butter
1 large onion
Cream
Brandy (optional)

Allow the chicken livers to completely defrost.

Chop the large onion and keep some in reserve for later.

Melt approximately 4 oz of butter and add the livers and most of the onion. Mix well together.

Cook slowly until there is no red in the livers.

Remove from the heat and blend with the raw onion and any other raw vegetables you want to add such as celery.

Add cream, a little salt, black pepper and brandy, mix well.

Put mixture into a dish (or two smaller dishes). Melt the remaining butter and pour over the top. Leave in the fridge to set.

Serve as a starter or snack with a little salad and warm toast.

Options: Instead of brandy you could use red wine.
              When adding the cream etc. add some whole peppercorns.

SALMON HERB PARCELS
DALE WINTON

4 Salmon steaks
2 oz butter
2 bay leaves
4 sprigs of parsley
4 onion slices
4 slivers of lemon rind
1 teaspoon of dried thyme
Salt and freshly ground black pepper
Watercress sprigs to finish

Put each salmon steak on a square of foil, large enough to wrap round the steak. Put a knob of butter on each steak plus half a bay leaf, one sprig of parsley, one slice of onion, one sliver of lemon rind and the dried thyme. Season to taste. Wrap the steaks in the foil and put into an ovenproof dish. Barely cover the bottom of the dish with water and bake in a moderate oven Gas 4/350°F/180°C for 15-20 minutes until the salmon is tender. Test with a fork when the flesh should flake easily. Unwrap the parcels and serve, garnish with watercress.

Dale xx

CHIP BUTTIE
TERRY WOGAN

Take two thick slices of crusty white bread.
Spread both slices liberally with plenty of butter.
Fill with sizzling hot, freshly fried chips.
Season to taste.

EAT IMMEDIATLEY.

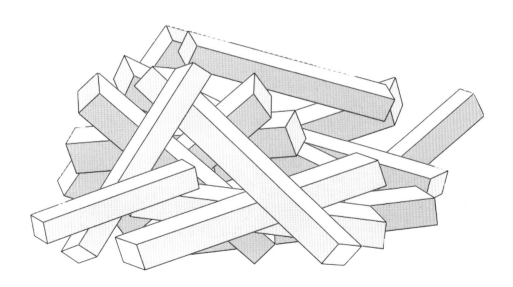

BEST SANDWICH EVER
Victoria Wood

Two big slices of wholemeal bread, preferably with bits in.
Bits of butter to spread on them.
Lots of avocado, tomato, cucumber, cress (alfalfa sprouts too if you live in one of the three places that sell them!)
Put it all together
(Put the bread on the outside)
Put real mayonnaise and salt and pepper in the middle.

Eat it.

Victoria Wood

CUMBERLAND SAUSAGES BRAISED IN RED WINE
RICHARD WOODALL

Serves 3

1lb (450g) pork sausages
1/2lb (225g) lean streaky bacon diced into cubes
1/2lb (225g) small button onions
1/2 teaspoon dried thyme
1 bayleaf
1 clove garlic crushed
1 heaped teaspoon plain flour
1/2 pt (275ml) red wine
6oz (175g) button mushrooms (slice if large)
Salt and freshly ground black pepper
Lard
Olive oil

Take a solid base frying pan or flameproof casserole, melt a little of the lard in it then add the sausages and cook until nicely browned.
Remove the sausages and set aside whilst you lightly brown the onions and diced bacon.
Then sprinkle in a heaped teaspoon of flour to soak up the juices and gradually stir in the red wine.
Return the sausages to the mixture along with the bayleaf, crushed garlic, thyme and a little seasoning.
Bring to simmering point then put the lid on the casserole and simmer very gently for 30 minutes.
Whilst the sausages are cooking, brown the mushrooms in a little olive oil ready to stir into the casserole.
Continue to cook for a further 20 minutes without the lid.

Serve with nice creamy mashed potatoes.

R.B. Woodall.

'GUYS THE LIMIT'

would like to express their sincere thanks to the following people without whom this book would not have been possible:

All the Stars & Celebrities who contributed recipes

Professor Alan Earnshaw - Trans-Pennine Publishing

Kevin Bradley - Burwain Studios

Barnabus Design & Repro - Truro

Reed's Printers - Penrith

Ullswater College Association

Staff at Ullswater Community College

The Shareholders of Guys the Limit

Our Advisors (especially Peter Ousby from A.R.C Conbloc, Blencow Brickworks)

Young Enterprise (Eden Board)

Crafty Baker - Penrith